COUNTRY · EXPLORERS ·

# A Visit to

# ITALY

## By Hermione Redshaw

BEARPORT
PUBLISHING

Minneapolis, Minnesota

## Credits

*All images are courtesy of Shutterstock.com, unless otherwise specified. With thanks to Getty Images, Thinkstock Photo, and iStockphoto.*

Cover – ermess, Yasonya. 2–3 – Yasonya. 4–5 – proslgn, Nerthuz. 6–7 – QQ7, Sean Pavone. 8–9 – S.Borisov, ecstk22. 10–11 – prochasson frederic, Yulia Serova. 12–13 – Grek Irina, Marina Andrejchenko. 14–15 – timages, Here. 16–17 – givaga, muratart. 18–19 – Public Domain, Arif, Pixel-Shot. 20–21 – Grisha Bruev, Alvaro German Vilela. 22–23 – f11photo, Kirill Skorobogatko, Raisa Suprun.

Library of Congress Cataloging-in-Publication Data is available at www.loc.gov or upon request from the publisher.

ISBN: 979-8-88509-972-1 (hardcover)
ISBN: 979-8-88822-151-8  (paperback)
ISBN: 979-8-88822-292-8 (ebook)

For more information, write to Bearport Publishing, 5357 Penn Avenue South, Minneapolis, MN 55419.

# CONTENTS

# COUNTRY TO COUNTRY

**Which country do you live in?**

A country is an area of land marked by **borders**. The people in each country have their own rules and ways of living. They may speak different languages.

Each country around the world has its own interesting things to see and do. Let's take a trip to visit a country and learn more!

Have you ever visited another country?

# TODAY'S TRIP IS TO
# ITALY!

ASIA

EUROPE

NORTH AMERICA

Italy

AFRICA

SOUTH AMERICA

AUSTRALIA

Italy is a country in the **continent** of Europe.

## FACT FILE

**Capital city:** Rome
**Main language:** Italian
**Currency:** Euro
**Flag:**

Currency is the type of money that is used in a country.

# ROME

We'll start our trip in Rome, the capital city of Italy! It has been around for a long time. Ancient Romans called it the **Eternal** City. They believed Rome would last forever.

Vatican City is its own country.

Vatican City is a small country inside of Rome. In fact, it's the smallest country in the world. It is an important place for the Catholic church.

# ANCIENT ROME

The Colosseum

Ancient Rome was built on hills known as the Seven Hills of Rome. It has many old buildings that are still standing today. The Colosseum was once used for **gladiator** fights and other contests.

The main language of ancient Rome was Latin. It's not spoken anymore, but many languages came from it.

# CULTURE

Much has changed in Italy since the days of ancient Rome. However, history is a very important part of Italian **culture**.

The culture in Italy is different depending on where we are in the country. Italians that live near the south or on Italian islands are often more **traditional**.

Culture in Italy is passed along in families.

# FOOD

Feeling hungry? Let's grab some pasta! The national dish of Italy is ragù alla Bolognese. It is known as spaghetti Bolognese around the world. *Yum!*

Eating in Italy is a social event. Dinners are usually enjoyed with family and friends. Whether at home or at a restaurant, the dishes are made to be shared with others.

# VENICE

Next, let's go to northern Italy to visit Venice. It is a beautiful city. Some of the world's greatest artists helped make some of the buildings.

One of the most interesting things about Venice is that it was built on water. We can ride a boat through **canals** to get around the city.

# ART AND MUSIC

Many famous artists are from Italy. Leonardo da Vinci was one of them. He painted the *Mona Lisa*.

**Opera** is a type of music that was created here. Many musical instruments came from Italy, including the violin and the piano.

# POMPEII

Pompeii was first uncovered nearly 2,000 years after it was buried.

Pompeii was a city built near the base of a **volcano** called Mount Vesuvius. In the year 79 CE, Vesuvius **erupted**. This covered the city and many of the people who lived there in ash.

People visit Pompeii to see the city frozen at the moment of the eruption. Some old streets and buildings look ruined, but others are in good condition.

# BEFORE YOU GO

We can't forget to take a photo with the Leaning Tower of Pisa! This leaning bell tower wasn't meant to be crooked. But after the third floor was built, it was clear that the tower was sinking into the soft ground.

We could head to one of Italy's many islands. There are more than 400 of them! The biggest island is Sicily. It is home to one of the tallest volcanoes in Europe, Mount Etna.

What have you learned about Italy on this trip?

# GLOSSARY

**borders** lines that show where one place ends and another begins

**canals** human-made waterways for boats

**continent** one of the world's seven large land masses

**culture** the customs and traditions shared by a group of people

**erupted** sent out lava, ash, steam, and gas

**eternal** endless in time

**gladiator** a man who fought animals or other men

**opera** a play in which all or most of the words are sung

**traditional** something that has stayed the same for many years

**volcano** a mountain that can erupt to let out hot, melted rock

# INDEX